TOZO HA1

What Makes These Budget-friendly Headphones a Game-Changer in Everyday Listening?

An Inside Look at the Features,

Technology, and Performance – Everything

You Need to Know

Joe E. Grayson

Table of Contents

Introduction

For those seeking quality sound without breaking the bank, the TOZO HA1 headphones have quickly captured attention as a standout in the budget category. With a reputation for durability, impressive battery life, and sound customization, these headphones have sparked the curiosity of both casual listeners and audio enthusiasts. Unlike many budget options, which often compromise on essential features, the TOZO HA1 strikes an unusual balance that prompts a closer look. At a glance, these headphones promise much more than the basic listening experience, and there's a growing buzz about what makes them a true value in an increasingly crowded market.

The goal of this book is to dive deeper, offering an inside look at what truly sets the TOZO HA1 apart. This isn't just a list of technical specifications; instead, it's a journey through the features, performance, and unique qualities that have made this model a favored choice among budget-conscious buyers. For readers wondering if a pair of headphones under $50 could genuinely deliver quality on par with pricier competitors, this book provides an answer, delving into each aspect with an engaging narrative that goes beyond the usual product review.

From outstanding battery life and straightforward Bluetooth connectivity to its customizable sound profile, the TOZO HA1 brings several impressive features to the table. We'll explore the design choices that prioritize comfort, the technology enabling its wireless stability, and the sound customization options available through the app, giving readers a clear understanding of what makes these headphones a unique and practical choice. By the end, you'll know precisely why these headphones have risen to such popularity and whether they can live up to their claim as a game-changer in everyday listening.

Chapter 1: The Rise of TOZO in Affordable Audio

TOZO has carved a distinctive place in the market by focusing on a mission often overlooked by premium audio brands: delivering quality at a price point accessible to all. Known for producing a range of audio devices that consistently offer solid performance at budget-friendly prices, TOZO has earned a reputation as a reliable choice for consumers who value both quality and affordability. Their approach sidesteps the high price tags associated with big-name brands, instead investing in practicality and functionality that resonate with everyday users. TOZO's commitment to balancing affordability with performance has made it an appealing choice for budget-conscious listeners who don't want to compromise on their audio experience.

As the demand for high-quality yet affordable headphones has grown, TOZO's strategy has only become more relevant. Audio enthusiasts have begun to seek budget options that go beyond basic functionality, wanting features like long battery life, comfortable design, and customizable sound without a steep price tag. The evolution of budget headphones reflects a shift in consumer priorities: a desire for advanced features without the premium cost. TOZO has addressed this need by focusing on the essentials that make a noticeable difference in day-to-day use—battery life, sound quality, and comfort—while keeping costs low.

The brand's ability to blend simplicity with quality is what sets it apart. In an industry where features like noise cancellation and high-end materials often drive up prices, TOZO's HA1 model remains affordable by focusing on practical, highly requested features that enhance the listening experience. This approach has positioned TOZO as a frontrunner in the budget headphone market, capturing the interest of users who see these headphones as a chance to enjoy great audio without overspending.

The TOZO HA1 model quickly drew attention in the world of budget headphones by striking a rare balance between quality and price. Unlike many options in the sub-$50 range, the HA1 doesn't merely cover the basics but pushes beyond, offering features typically reserved for higher-priced models. When it debuted, listeners were surprised to find a model that brought not only reliable sound quality but also impressive battery life, comfort, and user-friendly connectivity—qualities often sacrificed in budget headphones.

The standout appeal of the HA1 lies in its all-day battery life, boasting up to 70 hours of playtime on a single charge. This is a major draw for users who want uninterrupted listening without frequent recharges, whether for long workdays, travel, or simply extended listening sessions at home. The Bluetooth 5.4 connection, a dependable and stable upgrade from older Bluetooth versions, also captured interest, promising a smooth experience without lag or connection drops. This stability, paired with compatibility across devices, made the HA1 especially attractive for those wanting seamless integration with laptops, smartphones, tablets, and more.

Another key factor in the HA1's appeal is the combination of comfort and practicality in its design. With plush padding and a lightweight, foldable frame, the HA1 offers extended wear without causing discomfort—something often missing in similarly priced models. Its straightforward controls, designed for intuitive navigation, add to the appeal, making it easy to adjust volume, skip tracks, or tweak the EQ directly from the headset.

What initially set the HA1 apart, though, was its unexpected attention to detail in areas that matter most to everyday listeners. For a budget model, it achieves a rare mix of comfort, longevity, and practical features that resonate with a wide range of users, making it more than just another set of affordable headphones. In the HA1, TOZO managed to create a product that feels purposeful and thought-out, appealing to both seasoned audio enthusiasts and casual listeners looking for value without sacrificing quality.

Chapter 2: Unboxing the TOZO HA1 – First Impressions

Opening the box of the TOZO HA1 headphones, users are met with a straightforward, minimalist presentation that reflects TOZO's no-frills approach to budget audio. The packaging itself is lightweight, a nod to portability that aligns with the headphones' design. Inside, the contents are organized with the essentials in mind, providing just what users need to get started. Included is a USB-A to USB-C charging cable for quick recharging, a 3.5mm audio cable for optional wired listening, and a simple but informative quick-start guide and user manual. Though some may expect a carrying pouch or case, the absence of extra accessories is in line with TOZO's focus on affordability and practicality.

The lightweight packaging and minimalist layout make it clear that TOZO has prioritized essential functionality over excess.

The headphones themselves are designed with an emphasis on portability and comfort, making them an ideal choice for those on the move. Weighing in at a fraction of many over-ear competitors, the HA1 is easy to wear for long periods without causing strain. The foldable design adds another layer of convenience, allowing users to pack the headphones flat or folded up, fitting neatly into bags, backpacks, or even larger purses. This flexibility is a welcome feature for travelers or commuters who need a reliable, compact audio solution without added bulk.

TOZO's approach to design favors practicality: the lightweight build, foldable hinges, and unassuming aesthetics all cater to the needs of users looking for an everyday headphone option. Despite its compact size, the HA1 doesn't sacrifice durability. The frame is sturdy, capable of withstanding the usual wear and tear that comes with frequent use, while the padding along the headband and ear cups ensures comfort over extended periods. Together, these design elements reflect TOZO's understanding of what budget-conscious users prioritize, balancing portability and ease of use with a lightweight structure that fits seamlessly into an active lifestyle.

The TOZO HA1 headphones shine in comfort and build quality, offering a design that's crafted for long-lasting wear. From the moment they're put on, the plush padding on both the ear cups and headband make a noticeable difference, allowing listeners to settle in without the usual pressure points that can develop over extended listening. TOZO has outfitted the HA1 with generous cushioning that conforms well to the shape of the ears, providing a snug but comfortable fit. This is particularly appealing for users who need headphones they can wear throughout a full day of work, long flights, or hours of commuting without discomfort.

The lightweight frame adds another layer of comfort, as it minimizes any heaviness on the head or neck—a common complaint with larger, bulkier models. Even with extended use, the HA1's design prevents the kind of fatigue that can come from prolonged listening sessions. The headphones stay in place without clamping too tightly, striking the right balance between a secure fit and gentle pressure. This makes them suitable for various activities, from casual at-home listening to active use while traveling.

Beyond comfort, the build quality of the HA1 reflects TOZO's attention to detail in creating a durable, budget-friendly option. The frame is constructed to withstand regular use without signs of wear, and the folding mechanism feels sturdy enough to endure frequent packing and unpacking. Together, the lightweight structure, well-distributed padding, and durable frame make the HA1 a comfortable and resilient choice that meets the needs of everyday listeners. This thoughtful design allows users to focus on their audio experience without being distracted by physical discomfort, enhancing the appeal of the HA1 as a dependable companion for extended listening.

Chapter 3: Battery Life – Powering Through Your Day

The TOZO HA1's battery performance is one of its standout features, providing up to 70 hours of playtime on a single charge—a number that surpasses most competitors in the budget category. For those who depend on uninterrupted audio throughout the day, this extended battery life offers a level of convenience that eliminates the need for constant recharging. Real-world use has shown that the HA1 lives up to this claim; users report going days, even weeks, without needing to plug in, depending on their usage habits. This impressive battery life makes the HA1 particularly appealing for travelers, commuters, or anyone with a busy schedule who doesn't want the hassle of daily recharging.

When it does come time to recharge, the HA1's USB-C charging port provides a modern, efficient solution. USB-C has become the industry standard, offering faster charging speeds and a more durable connector compared to older USB models. This feature enables the HA1 to charge more quickly, minimizing downtime between listening sessions. For those who find themselves low on power but need a quick audio fix, the USB-C charging allows for rapid top-ups, getting users back to their music or podcasts with minimal delay.

In addition to its wireless capabilities, the HA1 also includes a 3.5mm audio jack, allowing users the option to switch to wired playback when needed. This feature can be a lifesaver in situations where the battery is running low and there's no immediate access to a charging source. The wired option not only extends the usability of the headphones but also offers flexibility for users who may prefer a direct audio connection for certain devices. This dual approach—combining long battery life, efficient USB-C charging, and a fallback wired option—makes the HA1 a versatile choice that easily adapts to the varying needs of users, whether they're on the go or relaxing at home.

In comparison to similarly priced headphones, the TOZO HA1 stands out with its remarkable 70-hour battery life, which far exceeds what's typically offered in the budget category. Many headphones in this range max out around 40 to 50 hours of continuous playback, making the HA1's longevity a key differentiator. For users who rely on their headphones throughout the day or over multiple days without the chance to recharge, the extended battery life of the HA1 adds substantial value.

This significant edge in battery life makes the HA1 an attractive choice for travelers, commuters, or anyone with a demanding schedule. Instead of having to charge daily or even every other day, users can enjoy a week or more of playback, depending on usage habits. This added convenience gives the HA1 a clear advantage over many of its competitors, securing its reputation as one of the best options for long-lasting power in the budget headphone market.

Chapter 4: Connectivity and Controls

The TOZO HA1 headphones come equipped with Bluetooth 5.4, which significantly enhances the stability and quality of wireless connections. This updated Bluetooth version ensures a reliable, lag-free experience whether paired with a smartphone, laptop, tablet, or desktop, reducing the interruptions and connection drops sometimes seen in older Bluetooth versions. With Bluetooth 5.4, users can switch seamlessly between devices, making the HA1 a convenient choice for multitaskers or anyone using multiple devices throughout the day. The improved connectivity allows for smooth audio streaming, making it suitable for activities like watching videos, listening to music, and taking calls without the frustrations of a weak or unstable connection.

The HA1's control layout further simplifies the user experience, with essential buttons thoughtfully placed on the right ear cup. This layout provides easy access to playback controls, making it convenient to pause, play, and skip tracks without needing to reach for the connected device. The volume controls are also located here and are intuitively designed to double as track skip buttons, offering a straightforward way to manage audio playback. Additionally, the EQ control button allows quick access to preset sound settings, letting users adjust their listening experience on the fly. This streamlined design means that users can effortlessly control their audio settings directly from the headphones, adding a level of convenience that enhances their practicality for everyday use.

One notable limitation, however, is the HA1's lack of a low-latency mode. While this doesn't impact general listening activities, it can affect users who are sensitive to audio lag, particularly during mobile gaming or real-time applications requiring precise timing. Low-latency mode is designed to reduce the delay between the audio and video, making it ideal for gamers who need near-instant audio response. Without this feature, the HA1 may introduce slight lag, which, while minor, could be noticeable to gamers who demand immediate audio feedback. Despite this limitation, the HA1's Bluetooth stability and intuitive control layout make it an excellent choice for most casual listening needs, providing smooth connectivity and ease of use across various devices.

Chapter 5: Customization with the TOZO App

The TOZO HA1 headphones offer compatibility with the TOZO app, adding an extra layer of functionality and customization that enhances the listening experience. Through the app, users can access a range of EQ presets designed to adjust sound quality to suit different preferences. These presets include options like Standard, Clear Treble, and Deep Bass, allowing users to quickly shift between sound profiles depending on their needs. This functionality makes it easy to enjoy a balanced audio experience right out of the box, with options to fine-tune sound without needing extensive technical know-how.

In addition to EQ presets, the TOZO app provides options for creating custom EQ profiles. For users who enjoy personalizing their sound, this feature allows adjustments across various frequency bands, making it possible to emphasize or reduce certain elements in the audio, such as bass, midrange, or treble. Setting up a custom profile is straightforward: users simply adjust the sliders for each frequency band until they achieve the desired balance. This flexibility in customizing audio allows for a truly tailored experience, whether enhancing dialogue clarity in podcasts or boosting bass for music genres that benefit from added depth.

Beyond audio customization, the TOZO app also enables firmware updates, ensuring the HA1 headphones are equipped with the latest features and improvements. Firmware updates are a convenient way for TOZO to refine performance, address minor bugs, or introduce enhancements to the device over time. The process is simple and user-friendly, allowing updates to be installed directly through the app. Together, these app features offer HA1 users easy access to sound adjustments and performance upgrades, making the TOZO app a valuable tool for those looking to maximize their headphones' potential.

While the TOZO app provides useful features for the HA1, such as basic EQ presets, custom sound profiles, and firmware updates, its functionality is somewhat limited compared to TOZO's higher-end models and similar apps from competing brands. Higher-end TOZO models often come with additional app options, including advanced EQ controls and more robust sound customization, giving users a wider range of adjustments to fine-tune audio precisely to their preferences. In contrast, the HA1's app features are streamlined, focusing mainly on essential sound adjustments without the depth of control found in pricier TOZO models.

Another area where the HA1's app support falls short is in the range of settings beyond EQ adjustments. While the app provides a solid foundation for sound customization, it lacks features like noise cancellation controls or ambient sound adjustments, which are more commonly available on higher-end TOZO models and other brands' apps. Competing headphone models in higher price ranges often offer more interactive features, such as adaptive sound settings that adjust based on surroundings or detailed soundscapes for specific listening environments.

Despite these limitations, the HA1's app still adds value to the headphones by offering essential sound personalization in a simple, easy-to-use format. For users seeking basic customization and firmware updates, the TOZO app meets core needs without overwhelming them with complex settings. The streamlined approach aligns well with the HA1's goal of providing quality audio at a budget-friendly price, giving listeners straightforward access to the most requested features without the added complexity or cost associated with premium models.

Chapter 6: Sound Quality – Performance Across Frequencies

Out of the box, the TOZO HA1 headphones deliver a balanced sound profile that leans slightly toward a neutral tone. This setup aims to offer clarity across a wide range of audio content, from music and movies to podcasts and calls. However, the initial sound can feel a bit flat for users who prefer more pronounced bass or heightened treble. The neutral profile allows listeners to hear audio details without overwhelming bass, making it versatile enough for general listening. That said, some users may find themselves wanting a bit more punch in the bass or extra brightness in the highs, especially for genres like pop, rock, or hip-hop, where a fuller sound can enhance the experience.

For those who want a more personalized listening experience, the TOZO app provides several preset EQ options and allows for custom adjustments to the sound profile. Users can select from presets like Deep Bass or Clear Treble, which emphasize specific frequencies to match different listening preferences. By boosting the bass, for example, users can add depth to the lower frequencies, creating a richer experience for bass-heavy music. Alternatively, selecting the Clear Treble preset brings more clarity to the high frequencies, making it an ideal choice for genres that benefit from sharper vocals and instruments.

For even greater customization, users can create a custom EQ profile by manually adjusting frequency bands within the app. Those who enjoy enhancing dialogue in podcasts or movies, for instance, might raise the midrange frequencies to bring voices forward, making speech clearer and more defined. Similarly, those who enjoy powerful bass lines can dial up the low frequencies, creating a punchier sound that retains detail without overwhelming other elements of the audio. This flexibility in sound adjustments allows listeners to fine-tune the headphones to match their specific audio tastes, making the HA1 an adaptable option for a wide range of content.

The TOZO HA1 headphones offer impressive sound quality across a range of volume levels, delivering clear audio for both music and spoken content. At moderate volume levels, the HA1 provides a well-balanced sound profile that remains free of distortion, making it ideal for everyday listening. However, as the volume reaches 75% or higher, some users may start to notice slight distortion, particularly in bass-heavy tracks or when pushing the headphones to their maximum output. At these higher levels, the bass can become less defined, resulting in a somewhat airy sound that affects overall clarity. For most listeners, keeping the volume below 75% maintains a clean, detailed sound that performs well across various audio genres.

When compared to TOZO's HT2 model, the HA1's sound quality reveals some distinctions. The HT2, positioned as a more premium option, manages distortion better at high volumes, allowing for louder listening with minimal impact on audio fidelity. This is especially noticeable in the bass response, where the HT2 offers a fuller, more controlled low end without sacrificing clarity. Additionally, the HT2 has a more refined sound profile, making it a better choice for users who prioritize rich detail and depth in their audio experience.

While the HA1 excels in delivering quality sound at a budget-friendly price, the HT2 offers enhanced audio precision and a smoother experience at higher volumes, catering to users willing to invest a bit more for upgraded sound quality. For those who prefer moderate listening volumes, the HA1 holds its own, providing a balanced and enjoyable sound that meets the needs of everyday listeners.

Chapter 7: Microphone and Call Quality

The TOZO HA1's microphone demonstrates impressive performance, particularly for a budget-friendly model, as it effectively isolates the user's voice in various environments. The microphone has been designed to prioritize vocal clarity, making it a reliable choice even when background noise is present. In quieter settings, the HA1 captures clear, well-defined speech with minimal interference, ensuring that conversations and recordings come through accurately. When tested in noisier environments, such as a busy street or a bustling café, the HA1 manages to filter out much of the ambient noise, though some background sounds may still seep through in especially loud settings. Nevertheless, the microphone's performance exceeds expectations for headphones at this price point, providing a level of noise isolation that adds value for everyday users.

These capabilities make the HA1 well-suited for a variety of practical use cases. For phone calls, the microphone effectively isolates the speaker's voice, allowing for clear communication without requiring the listener to constantly repeat themselves. This is particularly beneficial for those who make frequent calls in environments where background noise is an unavoidable factor. The HA1 also shines in situations like podcast recordings or virtual meetings, where clear voice transmission is crucial. The microphone's ability to maintain vocal clarity makes it an excellent tool for users who rely on headphones for casual content creation or professional virtual meetings. Whether on a call, recording a podcast, or engaging in a video conference, the

HA1 provides a level of microphone quality that keeps conversations smooth and intelligible.

Overall, the TOZO HA1's microphone performance in diverse environments adds to the versatility of these headphones, giving users confidence in the clarity of their voice, regardless of setting. This balance between affordability and functionality positions the HA1 as a practical choice for those seeking headphones that excel in both sound and communication quality.

While the TOZO HA1's microphone performs well for a budget headphone, especially in handling everyday tasks like phone calls and virtual meetings, it doesn't quite match the capabilities of advanced or professional microphones. Professional microphones are designed with specialized hardware and often feature enhanced noise-canceling technology, broader frequency response, and high-quality audio processing that captures the full depth and richness of the human voice. As a result, professional mics deliver a level of clarity and warmth that's challenging for most headphone microphones, including the HA1, to replicate.

The HA1 microphone's strength lies in its focus on vocal isolation and basic noise reduction, making it highly effective for routine calls or casual recording. However, when compared to professional-grade microphones, its limitations become more apparent, particularly in high-noise environments or when capturing nuanced details. Professionals working in audio production, podcasting, or broadcasting would likely notice a difference in sound fidelity and clarity. For these uses, a professional microphone provides superior accuracy, depth, and consistency, especially in controlled settings where sound quality is paramount.

That said, the HA1's microphone quality still holds its own in the context of typical consumer headphones. It's a practical choice for users who need clear call quality without the need for studio-level audio, offering a strong balance of performance and affordability for everyday communication needs.

Chapter 8: Missing Features – What the HA1 Leaves Out

The TOZO HA1 is designed as a budget-friendly headphone model, and to keep the price accessible, it omits some of the advanced features found in higher-end headphones. Notably, it lacks Active Noise Cancellation (ANC), Transparency Mode, and Auto Pause/Play, features that are becoming increasingly common in more premium models. ANC would typically block out ambient noise through active sound waves, which makes listening in busy environments more immersive. Similarly, Transparency Mode would allow ambient sounds to pass through, making it easier to stay aware of surroundings while listening, a particularly useful feature for outdoor or commuter settings. Auto

Pause/Play, another convenience in premium headphones, would automatically pause the audio when the headphones are removed and resume playback upon putting them back on.

Despite the absence of these advanced features, the HA1 makes up for it with thoughtful design elements that contribute to effective passive noise isolation. The over-ear, cushioned ear cups create a comfortable seal around the ears, which naturally blocks out a significant amount of external noise. The padding is dense and contours well to the head, forming a barrier that reduces sound leakage and helps isolate the audio. While it can't replicate the level of quiet achieved by active noise-canceling technology, the HA1's design still manages to provide an immersive listening experience in moderately noisy environments.

This passive noise isolation is ideal for users who need to focus on their audio without being entirely cut off from the outside world, as it strikes a balance between clarity and environmental awareness. By focusing on this efficient, design-based approach, the HA1 offers decent noise reduction for a range of everyday listening situations, maintaining quality without the need for costly, battery-draining active noise-canceling technology. For users seeking practical, budget-conscious headphones that provide clear sound in various environments, the HA1 offers a straightforward, functional solution that leverages design to reduce background distractions.

For users who prioritize advanced features like Active Noise Cancellation (ANC), Transparency Mode, or additional sound customization options, TOZO offers alternative models that cater to these needs—particularly the TOZO HT2. Positioned as a step up from the HA1, the HT2 includes ANC capabilities, enabling it to actively reduce background noise and deliver a more immersive audio experience, even in louder environments. This makes the HT2 a suitable option for users frequently in bustling settings, such as public transit or crowded spaces, where ANC can help maintain audio clarity.

In addition to ANC, the HT2 provides a richer array of sound modes and more customizable EQ settings, appealing to those who appreciate fine-tuning their audio. With the HT2, users can easily adjust the sound profile to emphasize specific frequencies, making it an excellent choice for those who prefer personalized audio settings. The added transparency mode also allows users to stay aware of their surroundings, offering a level of convenience and safety that can be beneficial for outdoor use.

While the HA1 meets essential needs at an affordable price, the HT2 caters to those who are willing to invest a bit more for a premium experience. Its enhanced feature set, including ANC and advanced sound modes, is ideal for users seeking a balance between high functionality and robust sound quality. For listeners who want greater control over their listening environment and audio experience, the HT2 presents an excellent alternative to the HA1 within TOZO's lineup, offering a level of versatility suited to a more diverse range of settings and preferences.

Chapter 9: User Reviews and Real-World Feedback

The TOZO HA1 has received largely positive feedback from users, particularly for its impressive battery life, sound quality, and comfort—all standout points in the budget headphone category. Many reviewers praise the HA1's ability to deliver up to 70 hours of playback, a feature that exceeds typical expectations for headphones in this price range. Users appreciate the convenience of not needing to recharge frequently, especially when using the HA1 for long workdays or travel. The comfort of the HA1 also garners favorable comments, with its lightweight, padded design allowing for extended wear without discomfort, a quality many users report as surprisingly good for its price.

Sound quality is another area where the HA1 meets and often surpasses expectations. While some users note the initial sound profile leans toward a neutral tone, the availability of EQ presets and custom adjustments through the TOZO app provides enough flexibility to suit a variety of listening preferences. Many users enjoy the balanced sound and commend the app's ease of use in adjusting the audio profile, although some wish for even more detailed customization options typically found in higher-end models.

In terms of aligning with TOZO's advertised features, the HA1 delivers reliably. The stable Bluetooth 5.4 connectivity, touted for its lag-free performance, is consistent with users' real-world experiences across various devices, with minimal connection issues reported. However, while the HA1 does provide passive noise isolation through its design, some users expected more advanced noise-canceling capabilities, especially given the growing prevalence of ANC in budget models. The lack of advanced features like ANC, Transparency Mode, and Auto Pause/Play is a common observation, though most users acknowledge that these exclusions are understandable given the HA1's focus on affordability.

Overall, the HA1 meets and, in some cases, exceeds the expectations of users looking for a dependable and long-lasting headphone option at an affordable price. Its strong battery life, solid audio quality, and comfortable design align well with TOZO's promises, making it a popular choice for those seeking practical, budget-friendly headphones that deliver on essential features without overpromising on advanced capabilities.

The TOZO HA1 headphones offer a well-rounded experience for budget-conscious users, combining essential features with reliable performance. Among their strengths, the most notable is the exceptional battery life, providing up to 70 hours on a single charge, a rare find in this price range. This extended playtime adds convenience for users who want long-lasting audio without frequent recharging, making the HA1 particularly appealing for travelers, commuters, and those with busy schedules. The lightweight design and comfortable padding further enhance the experience, allowing for extended wear without discomfort, which is often lacking in budget headphones.

The HA1 also excels in sound quality, delivering a balanced profile suitable for various types of audio content. While the out-of-the-box sound leans toward neutrality, users can personalize the audio with presets and custom EQ settings via the TOZO app. This flexibility is a significant benefit for listeners with specific sound preferences, especially given the model's affordable price. The stability of the Bluetooth 5.4 connection further supports a seamless experience across devices, allowing users to enjoy lag-free listening whether on a smartphone, tablet, or computer.

However, the HA1 does have areas for improvement, particularly in its lack of advanced features. The absence of Active Noise Cancellation (ANC) and Transparency Mode limits the headphones' effectiveness in noisy environments, making them less ideal for users who require immersive sound in high-traffic settings. The omission of Auto Pause/Play, while not essential, could also detract from convenience for those accustomed to these small yet helpful features in other models. Additionally, at higher volumes, the HA1's sound quality can experience slight distortion, especially in bass-heavy tracks, indicating a limitation in handling maximum output cleanly.

In balancing these strengths and drawbacks, the HA1 emerges as a solid choice for everyday listening needs. It successfully addresses core features—battery life, sound quality, and comfort—without overpromising on premium capabilities. While there are areas where it could improve, particularly for users seeking advanced sound management and noise control, the HA1 ultimately delivers a dependable and enjoyable experience for its price, making it a worthwhile option in the budget headphone market.

Conclusion

The TOZO HA1 headphones bring together a thoughtful selection of features that make them stand out in the budget headphone market. Among their strengths, battery life is particularly impressive, offering up to 70 hours of playtime on a single charge. This extended performance caters to users who value longevity and minimal downtime, whether they're on the go, commuting, traveling, or simply prefer fewer recharges. Comfort is another high point, with the HA1's lightweight design and generous padding allowing for extended wear without discomfort, making them suitable for all-day use. Additionally, the HA1's sound quality, supported by basic customization through the TOZO app, delivers a balanced and enjoyable listening experience, versatile enough for different types of audio content.

For users who seek a dependable, straightforward pair of headphones, the HA1 provides essential functionality without needing advanced features like Active Noise Cancellation or Auto Pause/Play. Those who prioritize the basics over extras will find the HA1 an affordable choice, offering quality where it counts. Casual listeners, frequent travelers, students, and busy professionals alike will appreciate the HA1's practicality, meeting fundamental needs without overloading the experience with unnecessary options.

The HA1's strengths are clear: it offers an outstanding battery life that keeps up with long listening sessions, a comfortable and lightweight design ideal for extended wear, stable Bluetooth

5.4 connectivity for seamless device pairing, and customizable EQ settings through the TOZO app that allow for a more tailored audio experience. These qualities provide solid value for basic audio needs, particularly given the HA1's affordable price point.

However, there are a few limitations to consider. The HA1 lacks some of the advanced features found in higher-end models, such as Active Noise Cancellation, Transparency Mode, and Auto Pause/Play. At higher volumes, users may notice slight distortion, especially in bass-heavy tracks, and the customization options are relatively basic compared to those available in premium models.

Despite these trade-offs, the TOZO HA1 redefines value in budget headphones by focusing on key features at an affordable price.

Instead of aiming to replicate high-end capabilities, it excels in the essentials: long battery life, comfort, and reliable sound quality. This focused approach has carved a unique place for the HA1 in the market, appealing to users who prioritize simplicity, practicality, and durability over premium features. For those who want dependable audio performance without a hefty price tag, the HA1 proves that high-quality listening can come at a budget-friendly cost.

www.ingramcontent.com/pod-product-compliance
Lightning Source LLC
LaVergne TN
LVHW051620050326
832903LV00033B/4590